The Emotional Abuse Recovery Journal

THE Emotional Abuse Recovery JOURNAL

Compassionate Practices to Reflect, Break the Cycle, and Heal

STEPHANIE SANDOVAL, LMFT

ROCKRIDGE
PRESS

First Rockridge Press trade paperback edition 2022

For general information on our other products and services, please contact our Customer Care Department within the United States at (866) 744-2665, or outside the United States at (510) 253-0500.

Some of the exercises originally appeared, in different form, in *The Verbal Abuse Recovery Journal*.

Paperback ISBN: 978-1-64876-299-4

Manufactured in the United States of America

Interior and Cover Designer: Lisa Schrieber
Art Producer: Sara Feinstein
Editor: Laura Cerrone
Production Editor: Jaime Chan
Production Manager: Jose Olivera

Illustrations © The Collective Studio/Creative Market

Author photo courtesy of Carlos Requenes/walkingphoto.mx

10 9 8 7 6 5 4 3 2 1 0

I dedicate this book to all my clients.
I am grateful for the privilege of
working and learning from each and
every one of you.

Contents

Introduction IX
How to Use This Journal X
Staying Safe XII

PART 1: IDENTIFYING EMOTIONAL ABUSE 1
PART 2: TAKING ACTION 45
PART 3: MOVING FORWARD 89

Looking Forward with Hope 135
Resources 136
References 137

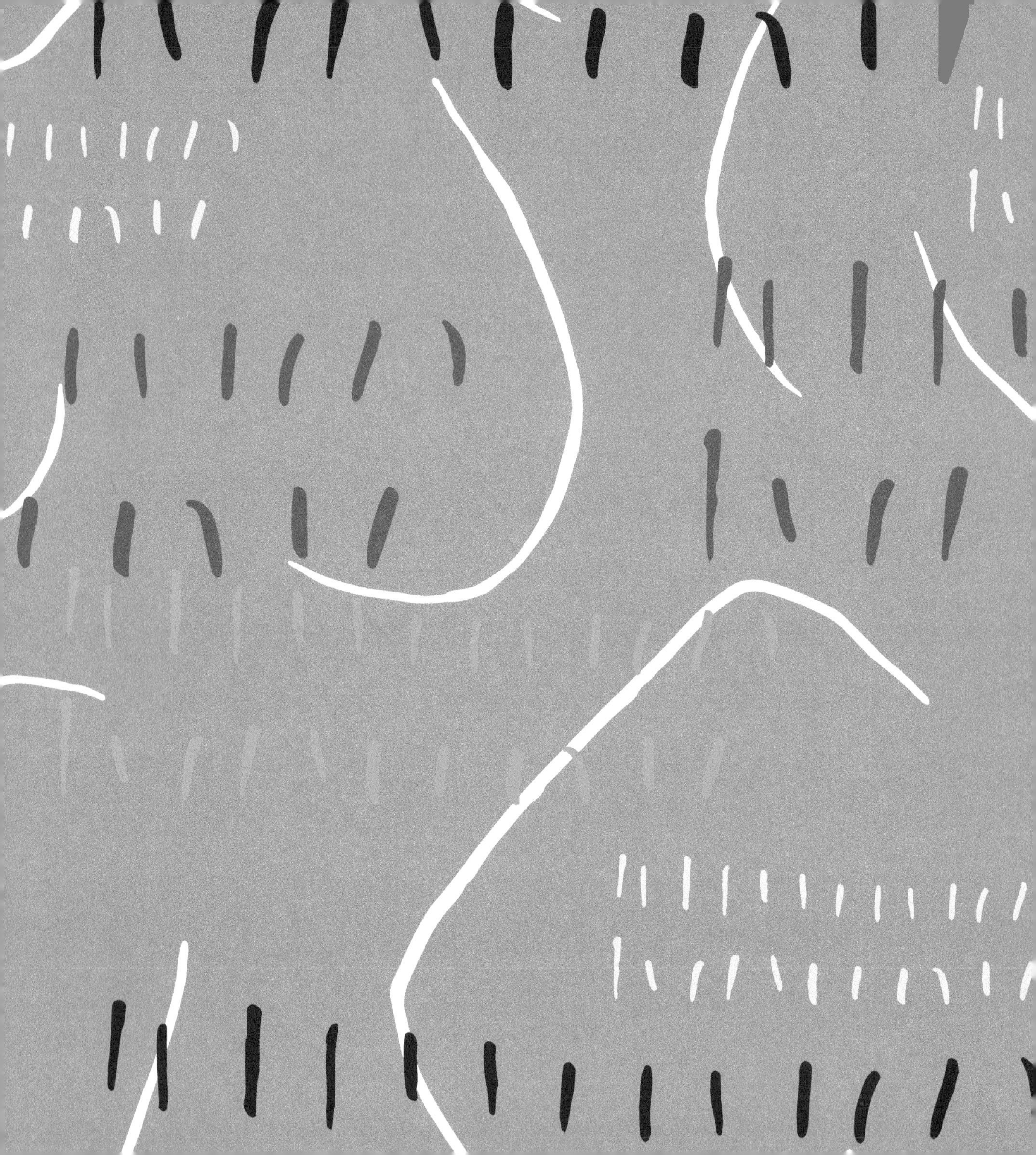

Introduction

Welcome to a space for guided introspection. A space where thoughtful self-exploration can transform into bold self-reclamation. I am glad you are here, because you matter.

My name is Stephanie Sandoval, and I am a Latinx licensed marriage and family therapist and the founder of Collective Space Therapy. I have spent years providing individualized and integrative therapy, as well as advocating for the availability of mental health services for all people and communities. I am passionate about supporting individuals on their journeys of self-exploration, reflection, and development. Extensive training and clinical work with individuals experiencing low self-esteem, depression, and trauma have allowed me to develop a creative approach to working with emotional abuse survivors by using a humanistic lens and an anti-oppressive framework.

This journal is a companion to *The Emotional Abuse Recovery Workbook*. These books offer a safe space to process the complexities of abuse and recovery and to navigate them through concepts and exercises.

I believe this journal to be foundational and imperative in the work of reclaiming your power and transforming silence into language and action. You will gain new perspectives on a path to healing. You will explore a deeper understanding of your current self and past self, and gain an expanded vision for your future self.

Emotional abuse is an attempt by one person to manipulate, frighten, control, or isolate another person, provoking confusion, fear, guilt, and shame within the other person. No one is immune to emotional abuse. Although it is a common occurrence in society, it is never acceptable and no one is deserving of it. Please know that you are not alone. This journal is the first step on your journey. Trust the process. It is never abuse that makes you stronger; strength comes from within you. You are powerful because you have the ability to heal and grow.

May you be met exactly as you are, wherever you are in time. All are welcome.

How to Use This Journal

The process of healing will look unique to each individual, and this journal can provide a helpful pathway for what to expect. There is no right or wrong way to heal, nor is there a time limit. There are no quick fixes in recovery; instead, it requires patience, intention, and an appetite for long-term perspective. Growth is not linear and can feel like healing and breaking all at once. There will be times when healing looks like taking steps backward, slowing down, and taking breaks. We all experience these moments. We heal in waves and spirals. Keep going. You have plenty of time when you tackle one thing at a time. The intention is to provide you with freedom to use this resource in whatever way works best for you. Some sections, prompts, practices, and exercises may feel harder than others, so feel free to skip and come back to them at any time. Some practices will ask you to use a separate blank notebook for ongoing work beyond the pages of this journal. Keep in mind that the nature of this journal can be difficult and triggering to work through. It's advised to reach out to a therapist for assistance. And although this book functions well as a standalone journal, please seek outside sources to obtain the necessary in-depth education required for emotional abuse recovery.

A Note to Our Readers:

This journal is an excellent way to work through a variety of different topics; however, any ongoing or debilitating symptoms of anxiety, depression, and other mental health concerns should be addressed by a medical professional immediately. The subject matter of this book may bring up difficult memories, possibly causing significant distress. Feel free to take a break at any time. If you recognize any complicated feelings and thoughts that could lead to the harm of yourself or others, please seek immediate assistance and call 911. This journal is not a replacement for a therapist, medication, or medical treatment. There is absolutely no shame in seeking help or treatment. You are not alone, and you are infinitely worthy of support. It is important to note that although a continual healing journey may work for some, it might not resonate with everyone. Healing is not meant to take over your life, and most people have to go beyond the self-reflection to really unlearn their internalized oppression. Scheduled therapy from a licensed professional can offer individualized support and guidance in a structured setting. Healing does not have a one-size-fits-all treatment, so feel free to experiment with various methods and always honor what works best for you. Resources for additional support can be found on page 136.

Staying Safe

Safety is the single most important priority in emotional abuse recovery, no matter where you are in your relationship. If you are reading this right now and feel like your life is in danger, please call local law enforcement immediately. Attempting to leave an abusive relationship can often lead to more abuse and may escalate to physical violence in attempts to maintain power and control, so it's imperative to reach out to a professional and seek out resources for support in keeping yourself safe. Please use the additional resources provided on page 136. It's likely that the abuser will not respond well to seeing this journal, so I advise you to be cautious and keep it hidden from their view. In addition, I recommend that you complete the first few prompts, practices, and exercises from each section on safety, and then continue to finish the journal as intended.

I wish to acknowledge the profound bravery it takes to enter this new territory. Treading into the discomfort of the unknown for the sake of truth is courageous. You are the hero of your own story. You have suffered from the pain of emotional abuse, and you are now admirably taking the steps toward healing and empowerment. I commend you for embarking on this daring new life chapter and building a strong foundation to hold the vastness of all that you are and who you will become.

PART 1

Identifying Emotional Abuse

Emotional abuse hijacks our well-being, leaves us unable to acknowledge or trust our emotions, and steals our ability to dream and have desires.

It's difficult to recognize emotional abuse, especially from someone close to you. Abusive behaviors can be covert or subtle, deceptive or direct, intentional or unintentional, conscious or unconscious. Always remember that abuse is never okay and never your fault.

The relationship we have with ourselves is foundational, and not acknowledging pain can have profound effects on our lives. In the short term, this can look like hopelessness. In the long term, it can manifest in depression, anxiety, disordered eating, substance abuse, PTSD, and chronic illness.

This section will help you identify emotional abuse, begin to accept your wound by naming your pain, develop emotional competency (the skill to recognize, interpret, and respond constructively to emotions), increase clarity, and fortify yourself with knowledge as you reclaim yourself.

Your safety is the single most important aspect of the path to healing. Before we start to examine your wound, it's vital to establish a space where you feel safe and comfortable processing the difficult thoughts, feelings, and emotions that arise during recovery. A safe space could be a physical place, an environment, or even the company of a person or group of people. Write about your safe space. How can you access it?

EMBODYING SAFETY WITHIN

As you begin healing, it's important to visit your sacred space often and learn what it's like to embody the feeling of comfort and find safety within. In this context, a sacred space is a secular place you regard with great respect that has personal meaning to you. When your nervous system is in a state of calm, you can attentively track your body's sensation from a place of mindfulness. The intention is to become an objective observer of what is happening within. Go to your sacred safe space and practice tracking your body's sensations with the following steps:

1. Find a comfortable sensation. This is a sensation that makes you feel safe.
2. Track and notice the sensation. Where do you feel it in your body?
3. Sit with and befriend the sensation. Sit with whatever comes up. Allow it to move through you. Does this sensation have a shape, form, or color? What is it saying?
4. Embody the sensation. As you remember these sensations, how do you know that you feel safe? What physical sensations are you associating with this feeling? As you become more aware of these sensations, how does this make you feel?

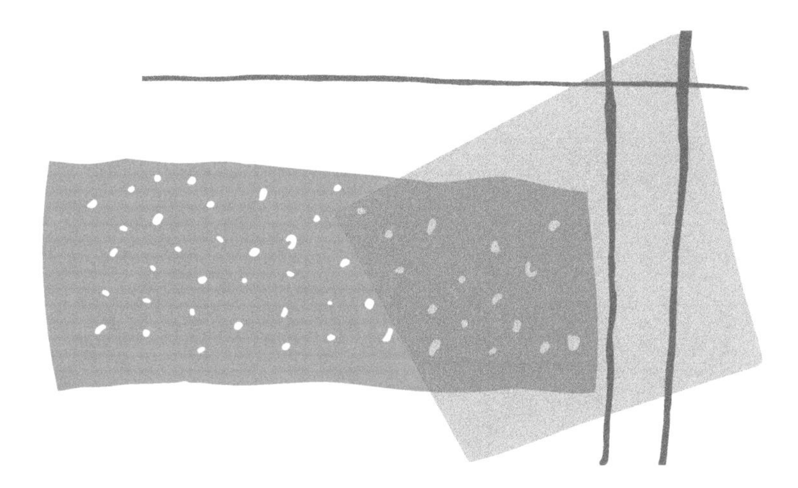

Acknowledging the wounds from emotional abuse can be challenging because it forces us to enter an intimate yet unfamiliar territory within. Emotional abuse leaves scars that are just as painful and damaging as physical scars. Unlike physical scars, emotional scars can be invisible and go unnoticed; identifying the wound is the first step in recovery. Describe your wound. Imagine the wound on your body. Where would it be?

Acknowledging the existence of a wound can be genuinely terrifying. Along with the wound, feelings of confusion, anxiousness, shame, self-consciousness, and uncertainty can bubble up. It's painful to admit that we have been harmed. When you think about the word *victim*, what comes to mind? How would you feel about identifying with that term?

Society has come a long way, but there is still a stigma toward talking about mental health. Perhaps this stigma may have prevented you from fully acknowledging your wound. When you think about mental health, therapy, and medication, what stigmas come to mind that might have influenced you? What new beliefs can you adopt that will support you in recovery?

Defense Mechanisms and Coping Strategies

Cognitive dissonance is the experience of perceiving contradictory information, and it can make you want to adjust your belief about the abuser to make it consistent with the action. It's common to cope from this with these defense mechanisms:

Denial: Declaring abuse to be untrue

Rationalization: Creating and constructing an acceptable reason for abusive behavior

Justification: Using explanations for why the abuse was right or reasonable

Learned helplessness: Conditioned self-blame; believing that the abuse is inescapable

Minimization: Reducing the pain; comparing yourself to others who "have it worse"

Fantasy: Hoping the abuse will stop or the abuser will change

This exercise can help identify ways these defense mechanisms have protected you in the past and how to integrate them into your recovery. Think back to moments after the abuse happened and write down something you told yourself to cope that pertains to each. Repeat each statement out loud with the addition of "and has protected me but no longer serves me."

Denial sounds like .... and has protected me but no longer serves me.

Rationalization sounds like .... and has protected me but no longer serves me.

Justification sounds like .... and has protected me but no longer serves me.

Learned helplessness sounds like .... and has protected me but no longer serves me.

Minimization sounds like .... and has protected me but no longer serves me.

Fantasy sounds like .... and has protected me but no longer serves me.

It can feel like a shell shock of overwhelming mental and emotional discomfort to try to process conflicting information and beliefs about the abuser. Cognitive dissonance is a coping strategy that protects you from the discomfort and anxiety these inconsistencies cause. Write about your experience with cognitive dissonance. If you find yourself experiencing cognitive dissonance, how can you care for yourself in the moment?

Fear stimulates the nervous system and causes instinctual fight, flight, freeze, and fawn reactions to protect us from harm. When we are in fight mode, we move toward a threat with aggression; when we are in flight mode, we move away from a threat quickly; when we are in freeze mode, we shut down in front of a threat silently; and when we are in fawn mode, we try to please a threat to avoid conflict. What protective reactions can you identify with?

A Letter of Compassion

During the process of recovery, it's common for a part of yourself to experience feelings of frustration with the other parts of yourself and how you coped with the wound from emotional abuse. This is normal, and these defense mechanisms are instinctive and protective; you must give yourself grace and compassion for operating in survival mode. Think about the various ways you coped with emotional abuse. What thoughts and feelings come to mind? Do any feelings of frustration or regret come up? Write a letter to yourself acknowledging these thoughts and feelings, and then access a place of compassion within yourself. Think about what you would say, and finish the letter with love and kindness.

I matter. My pain matters. My protection matters.
My safety matters. Prioritizing myself matters.

Emotional competency is the skill of recognizing, interpreting, and responding constructively to emotions and is a key foundation in healing. When you hear the words *emotions* and *feelings*, what comes to mind? What did your family, culture, and society teach you about feelings and emotions? What feelings are you uncomfortable showing others? Think back to your childhood and recall how those feelings were handled. How can you make space to express them now?

Emotional Intelligence 101

Emotions are core dimensions of the human experience, and learning to prioritize them is critical in healing. Although the words *emotions* and *feelings* are used interchangeably, emotions are associated with sensations activated in the body through neurotransmitters and hormones released by the brain, and feelings are the conscious experience of emotional reactions we can name.

This exercise will help you develop awareness of your emotions and how you experience them in your body. As mentioned in the previous exercise, recognizing, interpreting, and responding constructively to emotions in yourself and others is an essential skill. Think about each feeling and write any sensations you might have experienced when feeling that emotion.

When I feel fear, I experience these emotional sensations in my body: ....

....

When I feel sadness, I experience these emotional sensations in my body: ....

....

When I feel anger, I experience these emotional sensations in my body: ....

....

When I feel joy, I experience these emotional sensations in my body: ....

....

When I feel disgust, I experience these emotional sensations in my body:

When I feel contempt, I experience these emotional sensations in my body:

Feelings are colorful and complicated, providing knowledge and context to the human experience. Sometimes feelings can be complex because you can experience multiple feelings at once. Identifying and analyzing your feelings can lead to clarity. Think about a recent experience with emotional abuse. Can you identify three feelings you felt to describe your experience? Now think about each emotion individually and write down any thoughts associated with the abuse. For example, if you felt sad, what about the abuse makes you feel sad? What do you think that sadness is trying to tell you?

Feelings as Information

When emotional abuse hijacks your emotional world, you may feel unable to acknowledge or identify your feelings. As you start to reclaim your inner world, it's imperative to learn that feelings are information, not facts, and thus they are neither "good" nor "bad." Paul Ekman has dedicated his career to researching emotions, primarily focusing on seven basic emotions. In this exercise, shame and guilt are included with the seven basic emotions because learning about the information they offer is vital to recovery.

FEELING	INFORMATION
Fear	Lurking danger
Sadness	Impending loss
Anger	Urgent plea for justice and action
Joy	Impending gain
Surprise	Unexpected event
Disgust	Contamination, toxic contact
Contempt	Substandard behavior or being
Shame	Not meeting your own standards
Guilt	Not meeting someone else's standards

This exercise will help you identify how you currently relate to feelings so you can challenge them with your new knowledge of what they mean. Complete this exercise by writing down what immediately comes to mind when you think about experiencing each of the emotions. For example: When I feel shame, I think I'm in trouble. Then reflect on what the feeling is informing you of by referring to the table. Copy the table in a notebook and continue to document your feelings to increase your emotional awareness and competency.

When I feel fear, I think ....

When I feel sadness, I think ....

When I feel anger, I think ....

When I feel joy, I think ....

When I feel surprise, I think ....

When I feel disgust, I think ....

When I feel contempt, I think ....

When I feel shame, I think ....

When I feel guilt, I think ....

Identifying feelings is foundational to emotional regulation. When we deny feelings, or have feelings about our feelings, our emotions can become stronger and last longer. When you think about identifying feelings, what comes to mind? What limiting beliefs do you have about identifying emotions that can be challenged, and what new beliefs can you adopt to help support yourself in your healing process?

GATHERING ACCESSIBLE TOOLS TO COPE

When we name a feeling, it re-engages our prefrontal cortex and becomes tamed, or regulated, allowing us to think more clearly. "Name it to tame it" is a strategy that can help us cope with overwhelming emotions.

Once you name a feeling, you can create space to connect with the nurturing part of yourself by using each of your five senses in times of distress. It's important to keep in mind that there can be growth and distress at the same time in this practice.

Write down three activities for each sense and fill a box with the things needed for each activity listed. If an activity can't be placed in a box, write it on a sticky note and place it in the box as a reminder. Practice naming a feeling and using something in your "toolbox" as a grounding tool to reconnect you with the present moment.

Smell (e.g., lighting your favorite candle)

....

....

....

Touch (e.g., wrapping yourself in a soft blanket)

....

....

....

Taste (e.g., eating your favorite snack)

Hearing (e.g., playing waves on a sound machine)

Sight (e.g., reading your favorite book)

EXPANDING YOUR WINDOW OF TOLERANCE

Learning about your feelings and emotions will take you closer to the pain you've instinctively protected yourself from to survive. The experience of new feelings can sometimes cause distress, but it's important to remember that this is a process of expanding tolerance and healing. As you begin to expand your window of tolerance for uncomfortable feelings—your space within where you feel safe to tolerate uncomfortable emotions—use this practice to improve moments of distress. This practice is inspired by exercises that help navigate intense emotion through dialectical behavior therapy (DBT), a type of cognitive behavioral therapy that focuses on mindfulness and acceptance.

B- **BREATHE:** Breathe in to the count of 4, hold, then breathe out to the count of 6. Repeat.

E- **EXERCISE:** Engage in intense exercise.

T- **TEMPERATURE:** Change your body temperature using ice or cold water.

T- **TALK:** Say encouraging statements to yourself like, "I am doing my best."

E- **ENVISION:** Visualize safe spaces where nothing can hurt you.

R- **RELAX:** Tense your muscles when breathing in, relax them when breathing out.

I trust my own reality. I know my body and trust my feelings. I validate myself.

The Emotionally Abusive Behavior Checklist

Emotional abuse is subtle and difficult to detect because it has many forms. When we see the signs, we can recognize the harm abuse causes and do something about it rather than focus on internalized feelings of shame or guilt. When you focus on the signs, it can empower you to feel anger toward the abuser rather than anger toward yourself. Use the following checklist to help identify emotional abuse.

- ☐ They attempt to define how you "should" feel.
- ☐ They are dismissive, judgmental, and hypercritical toward you.
- ☐ They disrespect your boundaries.
- ☐ They hold you responsible for meeting unrealistic/inappropriate expectations.
- ☐ They are demanding, possessive, and controlling.
- ☐ They are constantly yelling, arguing, opposing, or antagonizing.
- ☐ They blame you for their problems and the problems in your relationship.
- ☐ They get upset when you don't do what they want or don't hold their same beliefs or opinions.
- ☐ They bring up something negative from your past to justify their behavior.
- ☐ They bring up "gifts" or favors they have given you to invoke guilt.
- ☐ They give demeaning suggestions on what you should/shouldn't do, undermining your choices.
- ☐ They label you as selfish or needy for having wants and needs of your own.

Projection is a manipulative tactic used to assign unconscious or undesirable feelings, traits, blame, and accusations onto a vulnerable and empathetic person. Within that vulnerable person, these undesirable feelings become internalized as toxic shame. Healthy shame says you have made a mistake; toxic shame says you are a mistake. The latter is a belief that causes inner conflict, self-blame, and low self-esteem. Write down your experiences of receiving projection and feeling toxic shame. How can you challenge those beliefs that are untrue?

Gaslighting is a manipulative tactic used to create a false narrative by denying your experience, minimizing, or trivializing your feelings or thoughts. This generates feelings of uncertainty and self-doubt. Abusers gaslight by insisting you said or did something you didn't, and make you feel as though you're imagining things. Write down your experiences of gaslighting. How can identifying gaslighting help you in your healing process?

IDENTIFYING MANIPULATIVE DISTRACTIONS

It's important to recognize the manipulative tactics used by abusers to distract you from their behaviors. Learning to recognize them provides clarity in conversations rather than leaving you with confusion and doubt. Write down and study these tactics in your notebook. Note which ones might be easier or more difficult to identify.

- ☐ **Word salad:** Talking in long monologues using nonsensical conversations so you can't get a word in
- ☐ **Generalizations:** Using broad statements or blanket statements (e.g., "all people get angry")
- ☐ **Mind reading:** Misrepresenting your thoughts and feelings by putting words in your mouth
- ☐ **Pre-emptive defense:** Overstating their abilities to be kind or trustworthy (e.g., "I'm a nice person")
- ☐ **Playing the victim:** Appealing to an emotional response of compassion
- ☐ **Overexaggerating:** Overstating and emphasizing claims or events to instigate emotions
- ☐ **Moving the goal posts:** Shifting the criteria a person must meet to appease them (the abuser)
- ☐ **Changing the subject:** Shifting the topic back to your reaction, your flaws, or the past
- ☐ **Scapegoating:** Assigning unfair blame

Identifying Types of Emotional Abuse

There are many different types of emotional abuse. This exercise will categorize abuse by aggressive, passive-aggressive, and manipulative communication styles, but it's important to note that some abuse belongs in multiple categories. Learning each type can empower you to recognize when the abuse is taking place and to take appropriate action against it. Knowledge is power and essential in healing.

Think about each category and check which types you've experienced. Then write down any emotions, feelings, and thoughts that come to mind in the space provided.

AGGRESSIVE

- ☐ Fear inducing ______
- ☐ Patronizing tone ______
- ☐ Yelling ______
- ☐ Verbal assaults ______
- ☐ Threats ______
- ☐ Insults disguised as jokes or sarcasm ______
- ☐ Humiliation ______

PASSIVE-AGGRESSIVE

- ☐ Silent treatment ______
- ☐ Guilt-tripping ______
- ☐ Nitpicking ______
- ☐ Rejection ______
- ☐ Boundary crossing ______
- ☐ Shaming ______

MANIPULATIVE

- [ ] Destructive conditioning (conditioning that pairs celebratory events with shame) ____________
- [ ] Lying ____________
- [ ] Financial control ____________
- [ ] Isolation ____________
- [ ] Entitlement ____________
- [ ] Triangulation (recruiting others to turn against you) ____________
- [ ] Catastrophizing (bringing up worst-case scenarios to discourage you from taking opportunities that will help you succeed) ____________

The three general patterns of emotional abuse are aggressing, denying, and minimizing. The four stages of abuse are: building tension, an incident of abuse, reconciliation, and calm. Think about these patterns and stages. What comes to mind? Which patterns and stages are easier to spot and which ones are more difficult? How can understanding these patterns and stages help you in your healing process?

When we learn about what emotional abuse is, it often challenges the messages we learned from our family, culture, and society that normalize hurtful behaviors. What are some emotional abusive behaviors you thought were normal? Where did you learn this from? What new beliefs can you adopt that will challenge the normalization of abuse and help you in your process of healing?

As we arm ourselves with knowledge, it can be helpful to recognize the profile of abusers. Some profile commonalities include the inability to take responsibility, receive criticism, or self-reflect. They play the victim, are concerned about their image, have no desire to change, and have an unending need for validation. Can you identify some of these commonalities in your experience with emotional abuse? How can understanding these commonalities help you in your recovery?

Profile commonalities in families include unpredictable rage, enmeshment, zero to few boundaries, rejection/abandonment, complete neglect, and extreme overprotection. Profile commonalities in the beginning of romantic relationships include quick involvement, excessive affection and attention, preoccupation with your safety, bait and feign innocence, and luring you into a false sense of security. Can you identify some of these commonalities in your experience with emotional abuse? How can understanding these commonalities help you in your recovery?

REDIRECTING YOUR ATTENTION WHEN WE ASK OURSELVES "WHY"

Victims are oftentimes haunted by questions like, "Why would they do this to me?" The goal of the abuser is to assert power and control within the relationship. Although the motives vary, they can be driven by institutional beliefs, learned behavior through generational trauma, and beliefs of superiority. Oftentimes they give many reasons for the abuse or say it wasn't intentional, invoking feelings of compassion that overshadow and distract you from their behavior and your pain. It's important to understand that even though you might understand the reasons behind the abuser's motivation, abuse is never okay, it's not your fault, and it's always unacceptable. When your mind is wondering why this abuse is happening to you, this practice can help refocus your attention to the present.

- Recognize when the "why" thoughts occur.
- Slowly inhale and exhale for five deep breaths.
- Repeat to yourself, "No matter why this is happening, it's not okay. It's not my fault."
- Engage in an act of self-care.

People with personality disorders, such as narcissistic, borderline, histrionic, and antisocial personality disorders, are highly egocentric, and the disorders have been connected to emotionally abusive behavior. Egocentrism is displayed through a lack of empathy and respect for others, an overzealous display of status, a generous or false self-image, a false sense of stature, and a failure to see other points of view. What comes to mind when you learn about egocentrism? Can you identify any of these characteristics in others?

"Hoover maneuver" is a tactic abusers use to re-establish contact after a conflict or separation with excessive apologies, begging for forgiveness, declarations of love, getting others involved, or threats of self-harm. When you think about hoover maneuver, what comes to mind? Has this happened to you or someone you know? If you experience it in the future, what can you do to resist it while supporting yourself in the healing process?

I am knowledgeable. I am powerful.
This has nothing to do with me. It is all them.

After you endure emotional abuse, you might immediately experience feelings of confusion, fear, shame, guilt, hopelessness, or helplessness. Overwhelming emotions can produce physical and behavioral side effects like difficulty concentrating, moodiness, muscle tension, nightmares, racing heartbeat, and various aches and pains throughout your body. What short-term effects have you experienced? Have you experienced more emotional effects than behavioral or physical effects?

WHAT TO TELL YOURSELF WHEN CONFRONTED WITH GUILT TRIPS

Feelings of excessive guilt are associated with long-term mental health conditions, including anxiety, depression, and obsessive-compulsive disorder. Frequent exposure to guilt trips can cause a guilt complex, which is a persistent belief that you have done (or will do) something wrong.

Guilt-tripping is the manipulative act of instilling guilt and responsibility for something. Rather than directly communicating one's displeasure, the person instigating the guilt trip refuses to say what's wrong and acts upset. Overwhelming feelings of guilt can cause us to freeze up in the moment or want to do something to please the other person.

Say the following statements in front of a mirror repeatedly to yourself. This practice will help remind you of what to tell yourself when confronted with someone who is guilt-tripping you so you can make decisions that are best for you.

- I will not make this personal.
- I know my feelings matter.
- I know my voice matters.
- I am allowed to say no.
- I am allowed to ask for space to think.
- I am not responsible for meeting their needs.
- I am not doing anything wrong.
- I am allowed to walk away.

Trauma bonding, also known as Stockholm syndrome, is a survival strategy that involves developing positive feelings and a sense of loyalty to the abuser. The victim also desires to receive love, comfort, validation, and approval from them. Think about trauma bonding and write down any emotions, feelings, and thoughts you might be experiencing.

Research shows that those who have suffered emotional abuse as children unconsciously return to familiar situations, a phenomenon called "repetition compulsion." Repetition compulsion causes further suffering because the victim holds subconscious beliefs of worthlessness and believes they deserve the abuse. Sometimes avoidable pain is chosen with the hope that one can finally find peace and love by "fixing" difficult situations; one believes that at long last they can "make it right." Think about repetition compulsion. Write down any emotions, feelings, and thoughts you are experiencing.

The strength I had to survive is still with me today,
and no one can take that away.
I am healing day by day, slowly but surely, one step at a time.

Grief is an incredibly unique experience for every individual, just like healing. There is no right or wrong way to grieve. There is no timeline, no stages, no pattern. Grief is not linear. Loss is integrated, not overcome. Grief for a relationship is the loss of hope. What hopes, wishes, dreams, or desires do you grieve?

It's normal to want the abuser to change so the pain will stop. The grief stemming from hope can catalyze the recognition that there are some things you cannot change; it can feel like the terrifying experience of losing control. Although you can't change someone else or the past, you can change the present and future by moving forward. How has wanting to change someone affected you? What new beliefs can you adopt that will help you move forward?

Emotional abusers validate a part of us that loves to help, an admirable value within that defines humanity. It's common for victims to take on the role of a rescuer, feeling connected and needed by taking on the problems of others and believing they are responsible for or have to "fix" other people's feelings. What comes up for you when you think about losing the rescuer within?

A CONVERSATION WITH SHAME AND GUILT

When we recognize that abusers use shaming and guilt trips as manipulation tactics, we grieve some of the toxic thoughts and beliefs that are associated with the feelings. This practice will help identify and separate the false narratives that have been imbued by emotional abuse. Complete part 1 and part 2. Then repeat the two parts, but replace shame with guilt.

PART 1

- Imagine you are sitting next to an empty chair. Then visualize shame sitting in that chair. What does it look like? What is it telling you? What tone does it have?
- Name the feelings you are experiencing. Accept the thoughts that come up without judgment. Notice the sensations you are experiencing in your body.
- Ask yourself what you need right now. Provide comfort to yourself.

PART 2

- Imagine you are sitting next to shame again, but this time it's your turn to speak. What would you say?
- Name the feelings you are experiencing. Accept the thoughts that come up without judgment. Notice the sensations you are experiencing in your body.
- Ask yourself what you need right now. Provide comfort to yourself.

Giving Thanks and Moving on from Self-Blame

Self-blame can feel like a familiar yet inescapable abyss of shame and anger toward oneself. It can lead to learned helplessness, a coping strategy developed after repeated exposure to abuse. Victims become more vulnerable to self-blame by inherently having a strong internal locus of control, believing events in their life are primarily a result of their own actions.

Grief involves the loss of control and the belief that you are to blame. This exercise will help you address how self-blame has protected you and explore how to integrate it into your healing process.

Dear Self-Blame,

I know you when ______________________.

I think of you as ______________________.

You tell me ______________________.

You have given me power and control by ______________________.

You have given me attention and protected me by ______________________.

When you're present, I don't have to change ______________________.

When you're present, I avoid vulnerability because ______________________.

I now know you no longer serve me because ______________________.

Thank you for ______________________.

I will grieve you by ______________________.

I will now think of you as ______________________.

You will now help me in my healing by ______________________.

Sincerely,

____

It's understandable to want an apology from the people who have hurt you so you can gain closure. It's common for abusers to ignore, deny, or conceal the pain they've inflicted or to offer empty apologies. What does closure mean to you? How would your recovery be affected if you weren't able to receive an apology?

As you build up the courage to face the pain of what you went through and learn how to identify emotional abuse, it's important to integrate the past and present. If this is an ending of a chapter in your life, what would it be called? As you begin a new chapter with a new narrative, what will it be called?

I am not defined by what has happened to me.
I am in control of my own story.
I know that healing is not linear and has no timetable.
I am going at my own pace and doing the best that I can.

PART 2

Taking Action

As you begin to accept and process the emotional abuse experienced, you'll gain a greater sense of awareness within yourself to explore. When you focus inward, you give yourself the space to heal and feel a range of complex emotions, feelings, and thoughts. It's important to recognize that still standing after enduring immense hardship is a true testament to your strength.

Because abuse deprives us of our power to move toward safety, give ourselves compassion, recognize our worth, create boundaries, and care for ourselves, this section will help you learn how you can become your greatest ally. Progressing through your healing requires you to courageously reclaim your power through actions that are aligned with taking care of yourself. It can be an uncomfortable experience at first, but as you continue to integrate healthy actions that reflect your worth into your life, you take back your sense of self and protect yourself from further abuse.

Safety is your number one priority in this process. Oftentimes people will tell you to leave the relationship, but the reality is that it's not that simple due to the complexities, nuances, and dangers of each person's situation. It's common for emotional abuse to drastically increase after attempts to leave, resulting in the need for restraining orders against the abuser. Think about leaving. What would it look like for you to make safety your number one priority? Who would help you gain the necessary resources to ensure your safety in this process?

Create an Emotional Safety Plan

Emotional safety is the experience of safely expressing and coping with one's feelings and emotions. An emotional safety plan is an individualized and practical plan on how to remain safe from an emotionally abusive relationship.

This exercise will help you learn what to do when you experience an emotional crisis—an internal state of distress which triggers the mind and body to go into survival mode. In this state, you may have trouble accessing other parts of yourself that can help you navigate your way to safety. After completing your emotional safety plan, make a copy and keep it in your home or on your phone so it's easily accessible. For further individualization, contact a therapist or trusted person for additional support.

- Identify safe spaces in or near your home.
- Identify warning signs (emotions, feelings, or thoughts that inform you that you are beginning to get overwhelmed).
- Identify triggers (behaviors or situations that cause you to feel overwhelmed).
- Distract (things you can do to take your mind off the situation).
- Soothe (things you can do to calm your nervous system).
- Recall positive affirmations (supportive and encouraging truths).
- Call people in your support system.

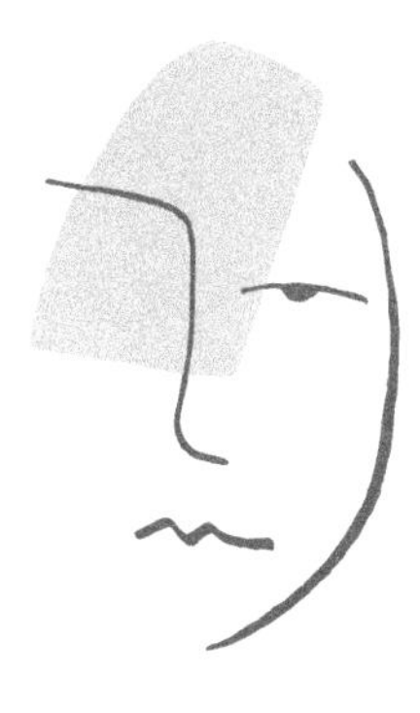

Self-compassion is the act of being courageously kind to yourself through the storms of healing as you are learning how to sail your ship. Compassion—kindness without any conditions—is a way to reclaim ourselves and our power during the healing process. How would you describe the part of you that feels compassion for yourself? What is your current relationship with kindness toward yourself?

Compassion is what we experience when we notice another person is suffering and want to help by providing comfort. Think about your childhood. What messages did you learn about compassion from your family? Were you shown compassion? Was compassion modeled by your family? What did your culture teach you about compassion? How can you adopt new beliefs to challenge negative messages you may have internalized about compassion?

A critical step in creating space within yourself for self-compassion is acknowledging your "inner critic," a harsh, judgmental voice that lives inside your head and has been internalized from the past. Judging yourself is a learned behavior. Who in your life did you experience to be very critical, judgmental, or hateful? What oppressive systems, institutions, or environments were you exposed to? How did experiencing them impact your life?

GENTLE REMINDERS FOR WHEN THE INNER CRITIC ATTACKS

Your inner critic can take on many forms. This practice will help you challenge attacks from your inner critic by exposing yourself to gentle reminders that the attacks are not justifiable and don't reflect your true self. Copy each response to a critical attack on a sticky note and post them in places where you will see them on a consistent basis.

Perfectionism: I'm allowed to make mistakes; perfection doesn't exist.

Toxic shame/Self-hatred: I'm committed to knowing I am good person; feelings aren't facts.

All or nothing: I am not defeated; nothing is ever black or white.

Obsessive worrying: It's okay to feel scared; I am not in danger.

Comparisons: I am not lacking in anything; unrealistic expectations do not serve anyone.

Harsh judgments: I respect myself; bullying is never okay.

"Shoulding": I will reframe "shoulds" into "wants"; I am not obligated to others.

Guilt: It's okay to feel fear and make authentic choices; anger in others doesn't mean I'm wrong.

Urgency: I can feel pressure and know that I have time; I am allowed to take my time.

Research shows that people who experience a high level of self-criticism could feel anxious when learning to be compassionate with themselves. What would it look like to befriend yourself by providing support and comfort when feelings of fear arise during this learning process? How would you kindly speak to yourself knowing these feelings can be part of this process?

We befriend ourselves by knowing and accepting ourselves while recognizing our common humanity. Think about yourself in a very honest way. What personal strengths and limitations do you have? What societal or economic privileges or disadvantages do you have? Think about common humanity. How can you remind yourself of your connection with other people, all of whom suffer at some point in their lives?

How to Let Go of Internalized Messages

Our inner critic is oftentimes triggered by situations or behaviors from others that induce fear and shame and that are associated with past projections experienced by abusers.

Projection identification is a relational process where the projection of one person is received by another and identified as their own. Recognizing this phenomenon can help us accept that, as victims, we experience a window of critical thoughts and shameful feelings of the abusers that are not actually our own. When we access compassion for ourselves during these times, it's important to validate our pain and redirect the anger to its rightful subject.

This ritual can help you release thoughts and feelings that have been internalized from abuse.

1. Identify what triggered you, what you're feeling, and what you're thinking. Write these down on three separate pieces of paper.
2. Reflect on this experience and validate your pain.
3. Put the paper with what triggered you in a box. This symbolizes getting to know yourself better, just like a friend would.
4. Take the papers with your feelings and thoughts written on them, hold them in each hand, and say:
    - "I see you and you are not mine to hold."
    - "It is not fair to hold you because you do not belong to me."
    - "It's disrespectful to myself to hold. It is not mine."
5. Now rip up each paper; this symbolizes release.

Our inner critic tells us we are inadequate and unworthy, whereas our outer critic is a hypervigilant voice within our minds that tells us the outside world is unsafe and untrustworthy. Think about your outer critic. How would you describe it? Where and when might it show up within you? What might it be holding you back from?

Meet Guilt with Kindness

Self-compassion can disrupt the cycle of guilt that spirals into shame. Kindness toward yourself creates space for self-reflection, helps validate your pain, and sets the groundwork for making healthy decisions.

Think about a time you experienced emotional abuse and felt guilty. Use this exercise to write a letter to guilt from your compassionate self.

Dear Guilt,

I sense you feel ______________________________ in my body.

When I feel you, I think ______________ and want to ______________________ to avoid disappointing others.

I know you are informing me that I have not met someone else's expectation, so I must ask:

What does this person expect of me? ______________________________

Is this expectation appropriate or reasonable? ______________________________

Because I value equality in relationships, is this expectation fair? ______________________

If I didn't feel guilty, what decisions would I make differently? ______________________

I am committed to knowing that just because someone feels disappointment with me, that doesn't mean I'm wrong, to blame, or am a bad person.

I am committed to freeing myself from the unreasonable or inappropriate expectations of others.

I am committed to making healthy choices that are aligned with my authentic self.

With love and compassion,

____

Toxic positivity and spiritual bypassing are practices that use optimism and gratitude to "rise above" negativity. However, they become barriers to accessing self-compassion by denying reality and dismissing or minimizing one's emotional experience. Write down any experience about how the pressure to stay happy and grateful has affected you. What messages have you received about "negativity," and what new beliefs can you adopt to help you in the process of healing?

HOLD NEGATIVE THOUGHTS WITH COMPASSIONATE CARE

What we don't express gets suppressed. Unprocessed feelings live in our bodies, making it more difficult to manage emotions and easier to act on impulses.

This four-step thought exercise is a way to show yourself compassion and respond to "negative" or critical thoughts with CARE. Think about a challenging time during your experience with emotional abuse—a time when you had negative thoughts but tried to stay positive. What were your thoughts? How did you feel?

C: **Consider** any thoughts with a compassionate lens and acknowledge feelings.

What thought is popping up? What are you currently feeling?

A: **Allow** them space and validate their existence as neither good nor bad.

How can you respond to the thought with validation, kindness, and nonjudgment?

R: **Reflect** on the reality of the situation and sit with any pain or discomfort.

What is the reality of the situation related to this thought?

E: **Express** acceptance.

How can you respond to your thought with love, compassion, and acceptance?

I am here to experience the wonder of my existence and accept myself, just as I am.

Reclaiming self-esteem is essential in healing. Erik Erikson, a renowned expert on human development, noted that achieving a solid sense of self—a well-defined identity that will lead to a life of consistency, stability, and security—is an important life task. A sense of self includes esteem, our inherent worth as a human being. How would you describe your self-esteem? How has emotional abuse affected your self-esteem? What would it look like for you to incorporate a life of consistency, stability, and security in your healing process?

Self-esteem is the ability to trust oneself. How much and in what ways do you trust yourself? In what ways do you not trust yourself? How has emotional abuse affected the way you trust yourself? What beliefs about trust can you adopt that will help support you during your healing process?

Counting on Myself with Confidence

Gaining confidence in your ability to meet your needs is essential to developing self-esteem.

This exercise is inspired by the "How Can I Resource Myself?" exercise commonly used in somatic therapy, a body-centered form of therapy that focuses on the mind and body connection. You will identify resources for yourself when you feel triggered and learn how to take steps toward safety. After you complete this exercise, practice actively using your resources on a consistent basis to gain confidence within yourself to meet your needs and keep you safe.

First identify what triggers your fight, flight, freeze, and fawn responses. Then think of what you need in those moments, what resources you have to meet that need, and how you can get your needs met.

My trigger: ....

My response: ....

I need: ....

Resources to help meet my need: ....

I can get my need met by: ....

My trigger: ....

My response: ....

I need: ....

Resources to help meet my need: ....

I can get my need met by: ....

My trigger: ....

My response: ....

I need: ....

Resources to help meet my need: ....

I can get my need met by: ....

Creating meaningful goals can be a catalyst for increasing your self-esteem and can pave the way to finding your unique purpose and passion. Think about your future self, the person you see yourself becoming as you heal. How would you describe your future self? What meaningful goals can you make that will bring you closer to becoming your future self during your healing process?

Failure can feel terrifying, especially when we take it personally. When your experiences of failure were met with harsh criticism, it makes sense that you would want to give up or not try at something. Self-esteem can increase when we learn that failure is a part of growth and an experience rather than a testament to your character. Humility allows us to admit and learn from mistakes. Think about failure. What does it mean to you? How can you integrate a supportive mindset and welcome failure as a part of your growth?

HOW TO BUILD BELIEF FROM WITHIN

Celebrating small victories is important to strengthening your self-efficacy—your belief in your ability to accomplish something. By acknowledging the accomplishment of small steps, you can increase your capacity for feeling joy and pride. Because pride is an emotion informing you of an increase in stature, whereas shame informs you of a decrease in stature, small victories can help combat toxic shame.

To work toward healing, start small and build on things you already feel somewhat confident in. Think of five small goals you would like to accomplish in relation to your hobbies, professional pursuits, or other personal interests. Then think of five practical steps you would need to take to complete each goal. After each step is completed, do something to celebrate your victory! Copy the following structure in your notebook to track the progress of your other goals.

GOAL: ______________________________

Step 1: ______________________________

I will celebrate by: ______________________________

Step 2: ______________________________

I will celebrate by: ______________________________

Step 3: ______________________________

I will celebrate by: ______________________________

Step 4: ______________________________

I will celebrate by: ______________________________

Final Step: ______________________________

I will celebrate by: ______________________________

Self-esteem requires the desire for respect from others. It's important to understand that before you can satisfy the desire for respect from others, you must first learn how to respect yourself. Self-respect is acknowledging the dignity of yourself, your inherent worth given to you for being born. How can you show up for yourself in ways that reflect respect for yourself during your healing process?

Universal human rights include the right to:

- Receive respect
- Say "no"
- Reject advice
- Establish personal priorities
- Express and protect feelings, needs, and preferences
- Protest unfair, disrespectful, abusive behavior
- Feel and constructively express anger
- Hold opinions that differ from others
- Ask for and facilitate change
- Create a happy and healthy life

> Write down any limiting beliefs that challenge those rights. Where did they come from? How can you integrate these rights into your healing process?

Engaging in activities driven by intrinsic values can help increase your self-esteem while supporting a sense of control over the experiences that influence your life. Intrinsic values include affiliation with friends, family, and community; connection with nature; concern for others; self-acceptance; social justice; and creativity. How can you integrate more joy into your life? Write down three activities you can engage in for each value that will help you in your recovery process. Then write down any thoughts and feelings that come up after.

I am a unique and valuable human being.
I know, trust, and respect myself.

WRAPPING YOURSELF IN BOUNDARIES ON A SENSORY LEVEL

Boundaries are essential to reclaiming your power and identity. They are guidelines you create to maintain your self-worth and identify respectable ways you would like to be treated by others. As you heal, boundaries help protect the sacred space within yourself with loving-kindness so you can continue to grow.

In developing healthy boundaries, it's important to learn that only you can provide the inner safety you personally need; no one else can do that for you.

This meditation practice is inspired by the somatic psychotherapy exercise, wrapping yourself into your own space to help facilitate your ability to feel boundaries on a sensory level. It will require you to have a light blanket.

1. Go to your sacred safe space.
2. Take your blanket and imagine it as a boundary, a protective shield.
3. Touch the blanket, mindfully describe to yourself how it feels, and notice your emotions.
4. Imagine the blanket is now an extension of yourself and wrap it around your body.
5. Allow yourself to feel this protective boundary, and notice what emotions you are experiencing.
6. Take the blanket off, notice how you feel, and describe your body boundary.

Family of origin plays a significant role in how we think about physical, emotional, verbal, and behavioral boundaries. Think about your childhood and adolescent years. What kind of boundaries did your family have? Were they strong, rigid, loose, open, flexible, distant, close, fluid, or merged? Think about each immediate family member and describe their boundaries. What messages were you given from your family beliefs of boundaries?

What beliefs have you internalized that have caused you to feel guilt when thinking about setting boundaries? (For example: Boundaries will threaten my relationships; boundaries will be unacceptable to others; boundaries are selfish.) What new beliefs can empower and support you in feeling confident when setting boundaries in the future? (For example: Boundaries are a form of self-respect; boundaries will help me heal; boundaries will help me build self-esteem.)

Healing requires you to re-examine your values and your heart's desires for how you want to interact with and relate to the world, others, and yourself. Boundaries help you live your values so you connect with your inner truth. Write down fifteen values that first come to your mind. It's important to understand that not everyone has the same values and this isn't a test. Then write down any emotions, feelings, or thoughts you experienced after completing this exercise.

Codependency and the Influence of Boundaries

Codependency is a psychological concept that refers to an enmeshed, overly connected relationship in which one person compromises their authentic self by valuing the other person's emotions, feelings, thoughts, needs, and desires above their own.

It's important to note that there are cultural and gender-based biases toward what constitutes codependent behavior and codependency. In this journal, we will refer to behaviors related to the abuse of power in relationships and systemic oppression.

Sometimes your values aren't in alignment with what is right for you. Your society, culture, family, and others could have been very influential in your formative years, causing you to internalize values that are not necessarily your own.

This exercise will help you identify any external values you may have internalized. Write down ten different values for each category, then circle each one you value as well. Examine the relationship between these values in order to create clarity and insight into limiting beliefs you may have adopted in life.

Family	**Cultural**	**Societal**

Healthy boundaries allow you to trust yourself, gain respect for yourself, protect yourself from physical and emotional intrusion, help you make choices that align with your authentic self, and empower you to take responsibility for your life. How would your life be different with healthy boundaries? What would you need to have healthy boundaries? How could healthy boundaries help your future?

How to Set Boundaries

Boundaries help separate your emotions, feelings, and thoughts from other people's emotions, feelings, and thoughts. Setting boundaries helps you communicate your needs and establish limits in relationships.

Inspired by a dialectical behavior therapy skill, this exercise is an interpersonal effectiveness tool that outlines a strategy to set healthy boundaries during the process of healing. Imagine a situation where you would like to set a boundary with someone in the future and write down the following:

S: State your observations of their behavior objectively.

T: Tell them how their behavior made you feel using "I" statements.

E: Express your boundary, assertively ask for what you want or need, or clearly say "no."

P: Present positive ways of how getting what you need or want will make you feel safe and help the relationship.

U: Use mindfulness. Check in with yourself. How are you feeling? How is your posture?

P: Plan to negotiate. Know your limits of what you're willing to accept or compromise. Plan to disengage if they are using manipulative tactics like projection or gaslighting.

The fear of rejection, abandonment, and confrontation can make it difficult to set boundaries. These barriers protect us from feeling vulnerable and exposed. Think about these three different fears. If they were to each happen, how would you feel and what would you think? What does confrontation mean to you? Write down any emotions, feelings, and thoughts that may be popping up.

A GUIDED MEDITATION FOR REDRAWING BOUNDARIES

Personal boundaries can be seen as property lines that separates where you end and someone else begins. It's normal to see "no trespassing" signs or messages conveying that there will be consequences if trespassing occurs.

This practice will help guide you in re-establishing your boundaries when they have been violated or trespassed.

1. Imagine your body as a house with a yard. What do you need to feel safe? Think of five things you need to feel safe.
2. Visualize a fence surrounding your house. The fence represents your personal boundaries to feel safe.
3. Imagine the other person as a neighboring house that you want to set a boundary with. What can you say to them to state your boundary? What do you need from them? How can they respect your boundary?
4. Visualize telling them what you need from them to honor your boundary. What will you no longer do out of respect for your boundary, and what are the consequences that will take place if your boundary is violated?

May I courageously set and maintain boundaries that reflect, advocate for, and protect my worth.

As we heal from emotional abuse, it's important to learn about communication. Communication styles include assertive, passive, passive-aggressive, aggressive, and manipulative. Think about your childhood; how would you describe your family members' communication styles? How would you describe your communication style? How has your experience with emotional abuse affected how you communicate with others?

Assertiveness Training and Communicating Your Needs

Learning how to assertively communicate is an active way to strengthen your identity. When you are assertive, you are capable of respectfully communicating your needs, asking for what you want, saying no to what doesn't serve you, and standing up for what you believe is right.

This exercise was inspired by Dr. Thomas Gordon's "I-messages," an effective tool in constructing how to assertively communicate your needs and wants. Think about a time you experienced emotional abuse. Give yourself love and compassion for responding in the best way that you could. Now imagine yourself assertively responding with the following steps:

1. Listen: Actively listen and repeat what they said or reflect to them what they are doing (e.g., silent treatment).
2. Behavior: Describe their behavior.
3. "I" not "You": State your experience using "I" statements.
    - I feel (state your feelings)
    - I think (state what you think)
    - I believe (state what you believe, after behavior is continually repeated)
4. Effect of Behavior: Express how their behavior affects you.
5. I Need: State what you need for yourself.
6. I Want: State what you want from them.

Confidence is essential in learning how to become assertive. Confidence in communication is trusting your abilities to clearly express your feelings and needs with a calm demeanor. It's important to understand that assertiveness takes practice to build confidence. What would it look like for you to practice assertive communication? Who can you practice with? How can you access kindness to yourself while you practice?

FLASHCARDS FOR RESPONDING TO MANIPULATION TACTICS

It can be difficult to advocate for yourself with people who communicate manipulatively, but as you gain a greater sense of self, you'll also gain clarity in what to say. This practice will assist you in knowing what to say when confronted with manipulative conflicts. Create flashcards by writing the following statements on index cards and practicing them.

Gaslighting: Attempting to invalidate your reality

"I see your perspective is different from mine; we remembered things differently."

"I feel hurt by what you're saying to me; this conversation is over/I need space."

"I won't allow you to tell me how I felt; my feelings are valid."

Mind reading: Attempting to tell you what you think

"I hear you, and that's not what I said."

"I feel like I'm not being heard; you're putting words in my mouth."

"I find it difficult to engage in this conversation when you jump to conclusions."

Projection: Attempting to make you believe you are inferior

"I see things differently."

"I disagree. That's your opinion."

"I refuse to be responsible for that."

Taking care of your emotional, mental, and physical health is essential in healing. Self-care can be an activity that represents safety. Think about self-care. How would you describe your relationship with taking care of yourself? Write down any thoughts and feelings that come up and then list five different activities you can do to feel safe, care for yourself, and benefit your well-being.

When we commit to taking care of ourselves, we recognize longing for the care we think others should give to us or have given us. What comes up for you when you think about this? How can you show yourself compassion during this time? In what ways can you reclaim self-care and learn to care for yourself like you think others should care for you?

SCHEDULE RITUALS, BREAKS, AND REST

Rituals are self-care healthy habits that are practiced on a routine basis, bringing you closer to your vision of healing and wellness. Rest is also very important in self-care because it's essential to restoring, recharging, and revitalizing the mind-body connection.

This practice will help you integrate rituals and breaks into your routine. First, list three things in each category that you would like to take care of yourself.

Physical

Mental

Emotional

Social

Spiritual

Then list four things that take up a significant amount of your time and you could use a break from. Use your calendar, planner, or phone calendar and schedule one ritual and one thing you need a break from within a biweekly period. Then schedule a day of rest where you have no agenda. Remember that rest is productive in healing and never wasteful. It's important to start slow during the healing process. Whenever you feel ready, you can add more rituals and breaks as needed or desired.

Holding space for yourself is self-care. When you integrate the harsh realities of pain you've endured into the story of your life, you are courageously taking care of yourself. Think about holding this truth now. How are you experiencing this reality? What does this new reality mean to you? How can you care for yourself right now?

I am my priority. I have the power to actively care for myself.

PART 3

Moving Forward

Although the scars of emotional abuse can break you down, they also can build you up. They can give you the strength to persist through life's challenges and the power to advocate for yourself and others. As you heal, you will cultivate the ability to desire more for yourself, your relationships, and the world around you. You will grow a bold self-love while entering a new chapter of your life that is filled with hope and intent. You will begin to learn healthy ways of communicating while crafting genuine and meaningful connections.

As you take up action toward healing, the path forward might not always be clear. Even without full clarity on what the future holds, it is important to know that growth and happiness are possible. The healing journey takes effort, and this section will help prepare you for what comes next.

CREATING A LONG-TERM PLAN TO KEEP YOU SAFE

Leaving a relationship is often a complicated decision. There are many layers involved, and it is never just black and white. This exercise will help you prepare a long-term exit plan that prioritizes your safety. Envision possibly leaving in the future, and write down what you would need to do. Then write possible obstacles you might face and steps you could take to overcome them.

FINANCES:

Obstacle: ______________________________

Steps to take to overcome obstacle: ______________________________

EMPLOYMENT:

Obstacle: ______________________________

Steps to take to overcome obstacle: ______________________________

HOUSING:

Obstacle: ______________________________

Steps to take to overcome obstacle: ______________________________

TRANSPORTATION:

Obstacle: ______________________________

Steps to take to overcome obstacle: ______________________________

LEGAL:

Obstacle: ....

Steps to take to overcome obstacle: ....

HEALTH CARE:

Obstacle: ....

Steps to take to overcome obstacle: ....

CHILDREN/PETS:

Obstacle: ....

Steps to take to overcome obstacle: ....

SUPPORT SYSTEM:

Obstacle: ....

Steps to take to overcome obstacle: ....

Note: *Federal labor laws protect victims against abuse that targets a person's race, gender, nationality, age, and religion in the workplace, and some state and local laws protect against bullying. Many states also have laws regarding breaking your lease if you are in an abusive relationship.*

CREATING A SHORT-TERM PLAN TO KEEP YOURSELF SAFE

If you are currently in an emotionally abusive relationship, it's normal to feel powerless to escape heated and hurtful attacks. It might feel like everything you say just adds fuel to the fire. This practice will help you develop a short-term exit plan to assist you to safety when confronted with abusive behavior. Write your responses down in your notebook and share it with a trusted person who can help support your plan.

I can create boundaries by stating (state what isn't working, express needs) ______________

____.

I can avoid the abusive behavior by ______________________________.

I can refuse to engage in abusive behavior by ______________________________.

I can leave the environment by going to ______________________________.

- If I leave, I will go ______________________, and I will need ______________

____.

- If I need to pack a bag, I can hide it ______________________________.
- I can document the abuse by ______________________________.
- If counseling is agreed upon, my intention is to ______________________________.
- I can find available support and help by ______________________________.

As you heal, it can be difficult to feel safe and comfortable in the external world. Routine can trigger fears of feeling trapped and losing your sense of power and security. What fears do you have about routine? How can you challenge them? If routine can set you on a path to independence and empowerment, how can you integrate it into your healing process?

WE ARE NOT MEANT TO HEAL ALONE

We are not meant to grow in isolation. We were never meant to figure it out on our own. A crucial step in this process is to share your thoughts, feelings, and emotional experience with someone you trust in a safe space. This can be anyone in your life who has the capacity to emotionally support you without giving any advice, just being there with you as a witness. A licensed therapist is highly recommended as well as survivor support groups.

Think about sharing your story with a witness. Who comes to mind? Plan a time that feels right for you to share your story with a trusted confidant. Once you've shared your story, continue to seek support in other ways. Write down three things you can do to increase your community of support and implement them in your healing process on a consistent basis.

I will protect my peace as I pave
the way to where I want to be.

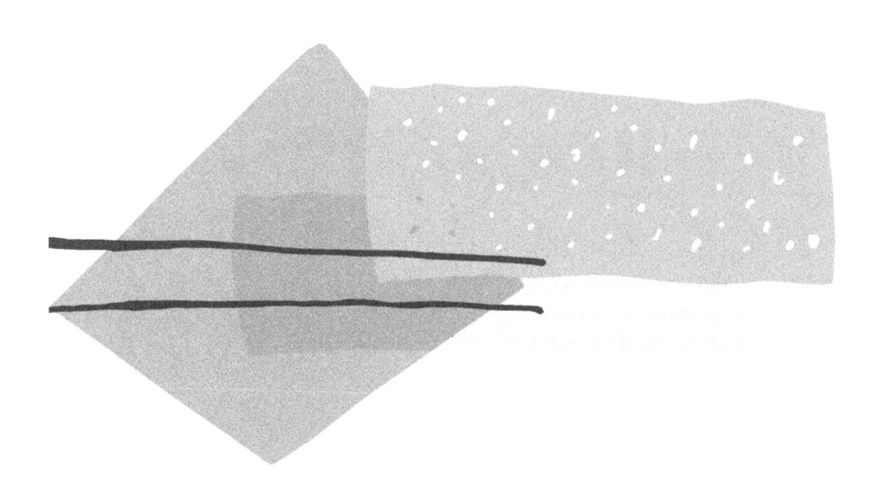

When you move forward, you pave the way for change within yourself, your future, and your future relationships. How would you describe your relationship with change? Do you embrace it or resist it? What fears come up when you think about change? How can you challenge them to support healthy change in your healing process?

As you heal, you'll begin to aspire to the dreams, goals, and ambitions you had for yourself before you endured abuse. Think about your current aspirations. Have they changed or are they the same?

A Letter of Hope for the Future

It's important to have hope for the future as you move forward. Take a moment to think about what your future self could look like and write a letter to them filled with hope.

Dear Future Self,

From,

Now write a letter from your future self to your present self. Think about if you had everything you wished and aspired for. How would you feel, and what would you think and believe?

If this exercise feels challenging, feel free to come back to it at any time during your healing. Because healing is not linear, you'll have days, moments, or periods that might feel like you're moving forward and others where you'll feel like you've taken ten steps backward. Remember to trust the process; you're doing a great job!

Dear Past Self (Your Current Self):

From,

Your Future Self

CREATING RITUALS AS A PATH TO START YOUR JOURNEY

Cultivating hope for ourselves and our future allows us to actively nurture our dreams in meaningful ways. Your future is crafted not only by your dreams and desires but also by what you do in your day-to-day life. The choices you make give you power to define who you want to become.

Habits are actions that become automatic, whereas rituals are how we mindfully prepare ourselves to perform habits. Rituals are a powerful tool in healing because they foster meaningful emotional connections and increase appreciation for what truly matters to you.

Think about an aspiration you have for your future self. What is one small habit you can do that will help you achieve your goal? Write it down in your notebook. Then think of how you can incorporate that habit in your daily routine and write down a plan to make that happen. Now think of a ritual you can do or tell yourself before you engage in the habit you're trying to create. This practice will help you create rituals that instill a sense of purpose in your life.

It can be difficult to think of aspirations for future relationships when you first start to heal from emotional abuse, but having a few goals can be helpful in the process of moving forward. When you think about aspirations you may have for future relationships, what comes to mind? Write down any emotions, feelings, and thoughts that start to surface.

As you challenge self-blame and move forward in creating new relationships, it's normal to experience moments when you don't trust yourself to choose a significant other who's right for you. Learning about what qualities you would like to seek in others can help you gain and build trust within. Think about five qualities you would want to see in others as you enter new relationships.

Research shows that when healthy relationships are based on honesty, trust, respect, and open communication, they help people live longer, deal with stress better, and have healthier habits. Think about healthy relationships and write down any emotions, feelings, and thoughts you might be experiencing. How has emotional abuse affected your perception of healthy relationships? How can you cultivate healthy relationships in your healing process?

CHEERS FOR FEARS: USING OPPOSITE ACTION TO GAIN CONNECTION

Emotional intimacy involves opening up to others, and it can feel scary trying to connect after experiencing continual verbal abuse. Fears of intimacy are often related to experiencing continual disappointment in relationships. Think about your past relationships with people who you've trusted and how you've experienced disappointment. What is it like for you to feel disappointment? What expectations did others not meet?

In dialectical behavior therapy (DBT), the opposite action of feeling the emotion of fear is to stay and do what triggers the fear. As you recognize your fear of opening up, you can seek out those you feel the most comfortable with to practice opposite action and become more vulnerable in your healing process. Think about someone you trust, and practice opposite action when talking about your healing process. This can be a trusted friend, family member, or licensed professional therapist.

Please note: During the early stages of recovery, only practice this skill while opening up with others who you already know you can trust.

As you begin to move forward and create healthy relationships, it's necessary to re-establish your expectations in relationships. Think about any current expectations you have of relationships. What do they look like? How has emotional abuse affected your expectations of relationships? Have your expectations changed? What do you want your future relationships to look like? What expectations would you re-establish with existing relationships?

Fostering Connections with Others and Yourself

Relationships are built on a foundation of friendship. This exercise is inspired by Dr. John Gottman's techniques to fostering healthy relationships. Use the three C's—curiosity, compliments, and constant kindness—as a tool to encourage mindful connections with others outside of this journal. But first, complete this exercise and write down your own answers to build a deeper connection with yourself.

Curiosity

Express interest in others by asking open-ended questions.

What is your philosophy on life?

In what settings are you the happiest or most comfortable?

In what settings are you the most unsure or uncomfortable?

During a typical day, what do you find yourself thinking about the most?

What is a major regret you have in life?

What is your greatest accomplishment to date?

Who is your biggest hero and why?

What are you most thankful for in this life?

What is the biggest lesson you've ever learned in life?

What gives you the greatest feeling of pride in yourself?

What makes something beautiful? ____________

What do you think happens when we die? ____________

Compliment

Express genuine compliments to others.

I love ____________.

I appreciate ____________.

I admire ____________.

I am grateful for ____________.

I am pleased by ____________.

I am delighted when ____________.

Constant Kindness

Express kindness often by doing these small gestures.

____

____

____

____

____

Relationships can become strained during the experience of emotional abuse. Think about the relationships you had with others before the abuse and write down how your relationships were affected.

Reaching out and rebuilding relationships is key in creating sustainable connections. Think about activities you can do with different people you'd like to foster a relationship with and write them down. What would it look like for you to implement those activities with the people you care about through your healing process?

I have the courage to step forward,
honor my vision, and achieve my dreams.

As you move forward in healing, it's important to learn healthy advocacy and build on your communication skills. Healthy advocacy is birthed from a supportive environment and trusting your abilities, characteristics, judgments, and insights. What would it look like for you to cultivate the requirements needed to have healthy advocacy?

When you advocate for yourself in a healthy way, you are mindful of how putting your needs first has an effect on others. This often looks like holding feelings of both anger and compassion at the same time. Think about holding these feelings while standing your ground. What comes to mind? What challenges might you face? What beliefs can you adopt that will help you hold those emotions while standing your ground in your healing process?

LEARNING HEALTHY RESPONSES TO DEAL WITH DISTRESS

Our fight, flight, freeze, and fawn reactions can become a barrier to healthy advocacy, so it's important to learn how to manage them during distressing interactions with others. This practice will assist you in learning how to move forward from the coping mechanism or mechanisms you use to protect yourself. In your notebook, write down three different ways you will help support yourself in moving forward. What new belief can you adopt that will help you in this process?

If you identify with the fight response, you can move forward by responding with boundaries and assertiveness.

If you identify with the flight response, you can move forward by disengaging in a respectful manner.

If you identify with the freeze response, you can move forward by cultivating mindfulness of your emotions, feelings, and thoughts in the present moment.

If you identify with the fawn response, you can move forward by approaching relationships with fairness, compromise, and negotiation.

Conflict is normal, natural, and ongoing in relationships. When conflict is rooted in trust and respect, it's constructive and can be a healthy way to strengthen the bond between two people. What feelings and thoughts come up when you think about conflict? What does conflict mean to you? What beliefs about conflict can you adopt to help you in your healing process?

To manage conflict effectively, we first need to manage our stress effectively. Stress management involves recognizing and managing your emotions. How do you experience stress in your body? What thoughts usually pop up? Do you experience stress often or seldom? As you heal, what would it look like for you to manage the stress you experience? What kind of support would you need?

BREAKING TOXIC COMMUNICATION HABITS

As we start to approach conflict as an opportunity to grow and strengthen relationships, it can be helpful to learn which communication habits lead to instability. Dr. John Gottman described communication patterns that destroy trust as "the four horsemen of the apocalypse." Although most people will fall victim to using these patterns from time to time, it's important to recognize them, make a repair, and work to use them less and less.

Write the following habits in your notebook. Can you relate to engaging in any of them? Write down any experiences you've had with each pattern and think about the remedy. What kind of obstacles might you face in trying to remedy each communication habit and what steps could you take to overcome them?

Criticism: Personal and characteristic verbal attacks

Remedy: Take a gentle approach; focus on the problem, not the person

Contempt: Intentional hurtful attacks directed toward personal worth and value

Remedy: State your feelings and needs; give compliments and recognize strengths

Defensiveness: Becoming the victim to deflect from blame or perceived attacks

Remedy: Take accountability for behavior; avoid blame or taking feedback personally

Stonewalling: Withdrawing to avoid conflict

Remedy: Agree to pause the conversation and engage in self-soothing activities

Conflict repair requires the ability to self-reflect and observe behaviors. As your sense of self increases, it becomes easier to use repairs such as sincere apologies, humor, curiosity, and problem-solving. How do you usually approach repairing conflict? How can you use these types of repairs as you build relationships in your healing process?

The Nonverbal Communication Checklist

Conflict management can be practiced by sharpening the skill to observe nonverbal communication within yourself and in others. Most human interactions are nonverbal, and only a small amount are verbalized. This exercise will help you learn the different types of nonverbal communication within yourself and others.

Observe yourself right now and use this checklist to track your nonverbal communication. Write down any additional observations in the space provided.

POSTURE:

- ☐ Upright
- ☐ Slouching
- ☐ ____________________

APPEARANCE:

- ☐ Tidy
- ☐ Disorderly
- ☐ ____________________

BODY MOVEMENT:

- ☐ Still
- ☐ Fidgeting
- ☐ ____________________

FACIAL EXPRESSION:

- ☐ Tight
- ☐ Relaxed
- ☐ ____________________

Think of a time when you conflicted with someone that hangs on your mind, and use this checklist to track how you experienced the other person.

USE OF WORDS:

- ☐ Monotone
- ☐ Dramatic
- ☐ ____________

TONE OF VOICE:

- ☐ High Pitch
- ☐ Low Pitch
- ☐ ____________

TALKING:

- ☐ Rapid
- ☐ Slow
- ☐ ____________

EYE MOVEMENT:

- ☐ Scanning
- ☐ Focused
- ☐ ____________

BODY CONTACT:

- ☐ Seeking contact
- ☐ Avoiding contact
- ☐ ____________

CONTINUED ON NEXT PAGE

CONTINUED

SOUNDS:

- ☐ Laughter
- ☐ "Umm, ahh"
- ☐ ____________________

SPATIAL USE:

- ☐ Appropriate
- ☐ Too far/too close
- ☐ ____________________

GESTURES:

- ☐ Expressive
- ☐ Non-expressive
- ☐ ____________________

When we start to set boundaries with others, especially with those who have emotionally abused us or with those who remind us of our abuser, it's normal to feel a range of emotions. We might feel proud one moment and then familiar feelings of anger, guilt, confusion, and loneliness the next moment. As you heal, how can you show yourself love and compassion while still holding your boundaries?

Using Humor to Challenge Your Inner Critic

Using humor to deal with obstacles is another skill that will help manage conflict. Humor, in the context of laughing with someone and not at someone, can be used to alleviate tension and reframe problems and perspectives.

Sometimes setting boundaries can trigger the wounds of the past. When this happens, you might feel overwhelmed, your inner critic might get louder, and you might want to re-engage in coping mechanisms that no longer serve you.

This exercise can help you challenge your inner critic with humor after you set a boundary. Take a few moments and think about setting a boundary with someone who might trigger you. What comes to mind? How do you feel? Now complete this exercise.

My inner critic says ....

....

I'm experiencing ...., which makes me want to cope by ....

Compassion says it's okay .... (validate feeling).

I understand how I would want to ....(coping mechanism) in order to protect myself.

Humor says .... (address inner critic with playful humor).

I know that boundaries will help me grow by ....

....

Knowing you have the right to say no is foundational to learning healthy advocacy. Saying no is a boundary that reclaims control of your time and energy. When you think about saying no, what comes to mind? What beliefs about saying no prevent you from advocating for yourself? What new beliefs about saying no can you adopt that will help you in your healing process?

I am a source of truth and honesty.
Communication is my bridge to advocacy and connection.

Self-love can mean many different things to different people. Write down what self-love means to you. What is your current relationship with self-love, and what would you like it look like in the future?

Love is fulfilling. When you love yourself in healing, your goal is to fulfill yourself as an individual. To do that, you must release the need to fill the expectations of others. When you release yourself from the expectations of others, you reclaim the power of freedom and self-respect. What expectations from others can you release that will help support yourself in your healing process?

Loving ourselves is a state of appreciation for our health, growth, and happiness. Self-love grows when we gain self-awareness and emotional competency through our process of healing. How can you prioritize self-awareness and emotional competency in your journey of self-love?

Attenuation is the urge to diminish oneself, to disappear, and to become invisible. As you learn to love yourself, you gain confidence to stand tall and take up space in places where you'd normally want to hide. Think about experiences you've had where you've felt small and write them down. Where were you and who were you with? Now imagine yourself embodying fierce self-love. How would you intervene and protect your small self? How would you take up space?

Learning Your Self-Love Language

Accountability is a foundational building block in self-love. When people are accountable in taking care of themselves, they can see the bigger picture and know what needs to change in order to foster self-love and take action.

Take accountability by learning your self-love language and show yourself some love. Quality time, words of affirmation, physical touch, receiving gifts, and acts of service can be categorized as different ways someone can express and receive love.

Write down three different ways you can express love to yourself in each language. Practice implementing these during your healing process, and write about your experiences in your notebook to understand which ones you value the most and the least. Create a self-love ritual with the language you value the most and practice it weekly.

Quality Time

Words of Affirmation

Physical Touch

Receiving Gifts

Acts of Service

Victims of emotional abuse tend to struggle with receiving compliments from others. As we heal and begin to love ourselves, we learn to embrace praise rather than reject it. What is your emotional experience when you receive compliments from others? How do you usually react? Think about a compliment you can say to yourself in this very moment; what is your compliment?

As we cultivate love for ourselves, we find joy in personal growth and challenge. Healing is about learning and unlearning. What do you want to learn more of as you continue your journey? What is something you are currently unlearning, and how has that experience been for you? What would you like to unlearn in the future?

Free Yourself from Comparison

> When we heal, we increase our sense of self and decrease the need to compare ourselves to others. Comparison can trigger emotional fear, highlighting uncertainty within yourself. Think about comparison and how it shows up in your process of healing. If you find yourself comparing yourself to others and feeling fear, how can you show yourself love and acceptance in the moment?

Who are you comparing yourself to? ....

What do they have that you wish you could have? ....

What would it mean if you had what they have? ....

Do you expect yourself to have this? ....

Where did this expectation come from? ....

Is this expectation realistic? ....

How can you challenge this expectation? ....

How can you show yourself love in this moment? ....

How can you show yourself acceptance in this moment? ....

What makes you unique? ....

How can you celebrate you as an individual? ....

....

What about yourself makes you happy? ....

....

How can you show yourself compassion in this moment? ....

Community care can be a way to foster fulfillment, connection, and purpose. There are many ways you can give back to others. Think about what it could look like to help someone out this week. Start small by volunteering your time to someone you're close with. What would it look like for you to volunteer your time and help your community?

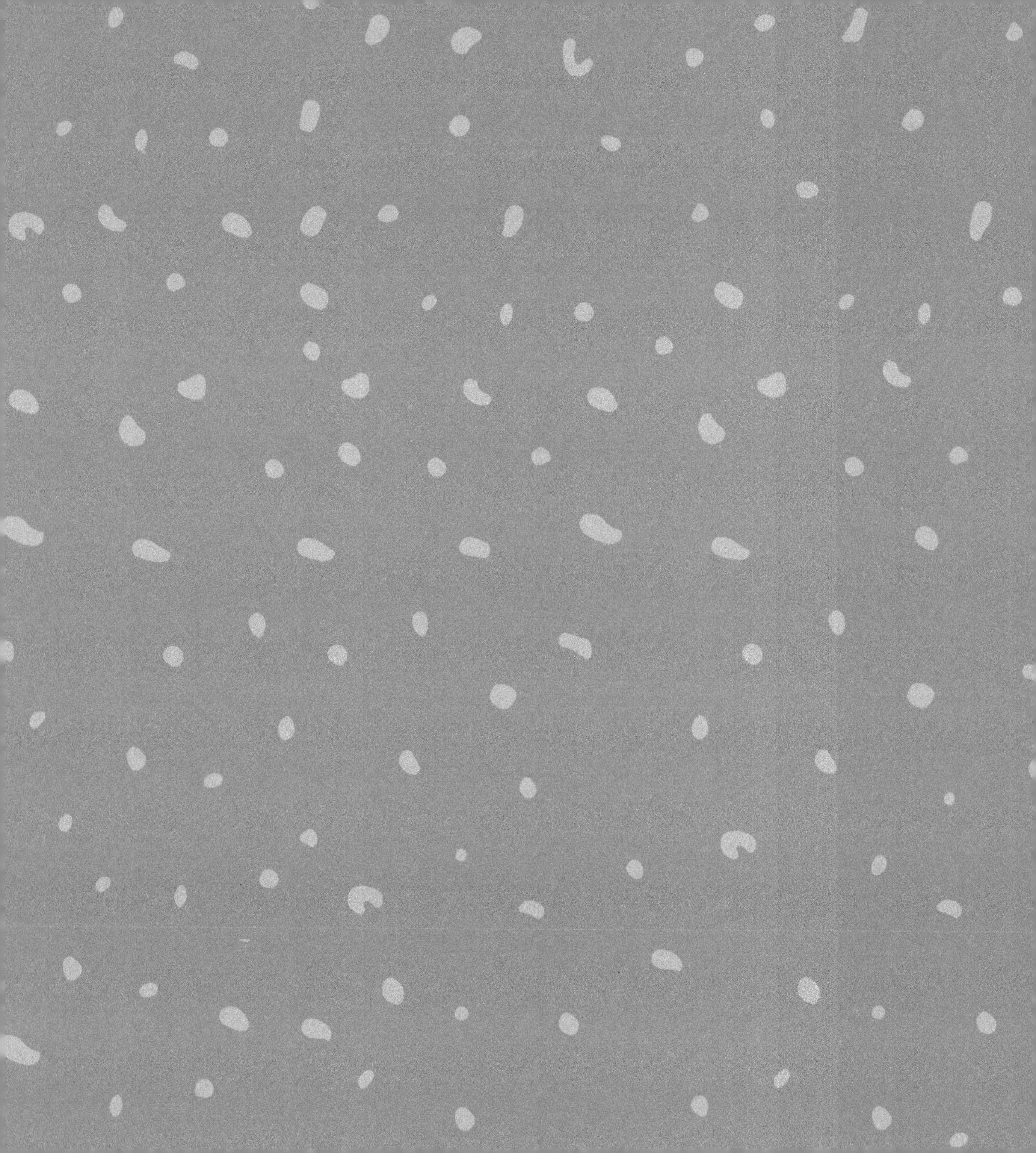

BUILDING COMFORT THROUGH TRADITIONS

As you deepen your love for yourself and your community, practicing traditions can help strengthen connections and bonds during your healing process. When you engage in traditions, you increase your sense of belonging and comfort. Traditions not only act like a glue that holds communities together, but they also support values of integrity, personal responsibility, freedom, and care for others.

Think about traditions and what they mean to you. Write down any traditions you currently have and traditions you would like to start in the spaces provided. What would it look like for you to practice old and new traditions? Reach out to your support system and community and plan to practice traditions during your healing process.

Weekly: ....

Monthly: ....

Yearly: ....

Food: ....

Clothing: ....

Holidays: ....

Entertainment (songs, dancing, games, celebrations): ....

....

Other: ....

....

....

Healing is an ongoing reflection of your past, present, and future. It's also important to understand that healing is not linear, a state of being, or an end goal; healing is a process that is unique to every individual. What would it look like to love and accept yourself during the ups and downs, the good days and bad days? How can you show yourself ongoing and unconditional love moving forward?

I can love myself and foster a connection with my community.

Looking Forward with Hope

Congratulations! You made it through this journal! Self-reflection is a courageous act, and your bravery is worthy of praise. As you continue this journey, remember you are going through a transition, which is not limited to yourself and could also include relationships, careers, health, and other things that are shifting in your life. During this transition, choose yourself and the rest will come later.

When you choose yourself, you create a space to look forward with hope. You will begin to understand yourself on a whole new level and set out to define yourself. You will start to create deep connections with others and your community of choice. You will embrace new challenges that may have previously felt impossible. You will find acceptance in all feelings that arise, and embrace them with curiosity and compassion. You will build trust and respect for yourself by continuing to practice boundaries and prioritize your needs. You will know the value of your voice. You will stop holding on to relationships that no longer serve you and stop trying to please others. You will make mistakes, as we all do, but you will do so in the absence of crippling guilt and shame. Instead, you will take responsibility for your actions and focus on personal growth. You will create safety within and live comfortably in your own skin. You will live by your personal values and endeavor for your own dreams, passions, and goals.

Through this continual practice, you are creating a powerful, finely tuned sense of self that is uniquely you, ready to embrace a fulfilling existence while finding a reservoir of peace within yourself, your community, and humanity.

Resources

These are national hotlines and websites that provide one-on-one support, safety planning, educational information, support groups, and additional resources. Note that if you are in immediate danger, please call 911.

National Domestic Violence Hotline:
1-800-799-SAFE (7233) / Text
1-800-787-3224
TheHotline.org

Day One—The Call to Safety:
1-866-223-1111
DayOneServices.org/verbal-abuse

Safe Horizon Abuse Hotline:
1-800-621-HOPE (4673)
SafeHorizon.org

National Teen Dating Abuse Hotline:
1-866-331-9474
LoveIsRespect.org

NATIONAL THERAPIST DIRECTORIES:

Psychology Today:
PsychologyToday.com

LatinxTherapy:
LatinxTherapy.com

Therapy for Black Girls:
TherapyforBlackGirls.com

National Queer & Trans Therapists of Color Network:
NQTTCN.com/directory

TherapyTribe:
TherapyTribe.com

The International Resource Center for Daughters, Sons, and Partners of Narcissists:
WillIEverBeGoodEnough.com/resources/find-a-therapist

References

Chapman, Gary, and Amy Summers. *The Five Love Languages: How to Express Heartfelt Commitment to Your Mate.* Nashville, TN: LifeWay Press, 2016.

Durvasula, Ramani. *Should I Stay or Should I Go?: Surviving a Relationship with a Narcissist.* New York: Post Hill Press, 2015.

Edmonds.edu. "Conflict Resolution Skills." Accessed March 27, 2022. edmonds.edu /counseling/documents/Conflict.pdf.

Ekman, Paul. *Emotions Revealed: Recognizing Faces and Feelings to Improve Communication and Emotional Life.* New York: Henry Holt and Co., 2007.

Erikson, Erik H. *Identity: Youth and Crisis.* New York: W. W. Norton Company, 1968.

Genesis Women's Shelter & Support. "Emotional Safety Planning." August 10, 2020. genesisshelter.org/emotional-safety-planning.

Gordon, Thomas. *Parent Effectiveness Training: The No-Lose Program for Raising Responsible Children.* New York: P. H. Wyden, 1970.

Gottman, John, and Nan Silver. *Why Marriages Succeed or Fail: And How You Can Make Yours Last.* New York: Simon & Schuster, 1995.

Greene, Robert. *The Laws of Human Nature.* New York: Penguin Books, 2019.

Mischke-Reeds, Manuela. *Somatic Psychotherapy Toolbox: 125 Worksheets and Exercises to Treat Trauma & Stress.* Eau Claire, WI: PESI, 2018.

Nicholls, Tonia L., Michelle M. Pritchard, Kim A. Reeves, and Edward Hilterman. "Risk Assessment in Intimate Partner Violence: A Systematic Review of

Contemporary Approaches." *Partner Abuse* 4, no. 1 (2013): 76–168. doi.org/10.1891/1946-6560.4.1.76.

Razzetti, Gustavo. "The Power of Rituals: How to Build Meaningful Habits." February 11, 2020. fearlessculture.design/blog-posts/the-power-of-rituals-how-to-build-meaningful-habits.

Siegel, Daniel J., and Tina Payne Bryson. *The Whole-Brain Child: 12 Revolutionary Strategies to Nurture Your Child's Developing Mind*. New York: Bantam, 2012.

Walker, Pete. *Complex PTSD: From Surviving to Thriving: A Guide and Map for Recovering from Childhood Trauma*. CreateSpace Independent Publishing Platform, 2013.

Warren, Ricks, Elke Smeets, and Kristin Neff. "Self-Criticism and Self-Compassion: Risk and Resilience." *Current Psychiatry* 15, no. 12 (December 2016): 18–33. self-compassion.org/wp-content/uploads/2016/12/Self-Criticism.pdf.

ACKNOWLEDGMENTS

I am not self-made. I am family-made, community-made, ancestor-made. I am made up of everyone I have ever known. Thank you kindly to every person who I've had the pleasure of crossing paths within this lifetime. I am who I am because of you.

ABOUT THE AUTHOR

Stephanie Sandoval is a Latinx licensed marriage and family therapist, founder of Collective Space Therapy, and author of *The Verbal Abuse Recovery Journal*. With extensive training and experience working with individuals experiencing low self-esteem, depression, and trauma, Stephanie provides a creative therapeutic approach to verbal abuse with a humanistic lens. Her practice reflects an active commitment to social justice and intergenerational healing on an individual, community, institutional, and global scale. Stephanie is a lifelong learner, driven by her innate curiosity and passion for exploration of self and others. With an anti-oppressive framework, she holds a vision for providing modern mental health services that reflect the values of ethical and sustainable wellness.